Taylor's Pocket Guide to

Ground Covers for Sun

Taylor's Pocket Guide to

Ground Covers
for Sun

A N N   R E I L L Y
Consulting Editor

A Chanticleer Press Edition

Houghton Mifflin Company

Boston

Taylor's Pocket Guide is a
registered trademark of
Houghton Mifflin Company.

For information about
permission to reproduce selections from this book,
write to Permission,
Houghton Mifflin Company, 215 Park Avenue South,
New York, New York, 10003

Based on Taylor's Encyclopedia of Gardening, Fourth Edition,
Copyright © 1961 by Norman Taylor,
revised and edited by
Gordon P. Dewolf, Jr.

Prepared and produced by Chanticleer Press, New York
Typeset by Dix Type, Inc., Syracuse, New York
Printed and bound by
Dai Nippon, Hong Kong

Library of Congress Catalog Card Number: 89-85028
ISBN: 0-395-52249-8

DNP   10   9   8   7   6   5   4   3   2

CONTENTS

Introduction
GARDENING WITH
GROUND COVERS FOR SUN
6

The Plant Descriptions
GROUND COVERS FOR SUN
25

Appendices
HARDINESS ZONE MAP
106

GARDEN PESTS AND DISEASES
108

GLOSSARY
112

PHOTO CREDITS
120

INDEX
121

GARDENING WITH GROUND COVERS FOR SUN

EXISTING in wonderful variety, ground covers are versatile plants that have endless uses and solve many problems. Imagine a cloud of Rock Cress cascading over a wall, or rolling hills carpeted in heather; picture a steep slope blanketed with Crown Vetch, red-berried cotoneaster lining a walkway, or shrub borders unified by the silvery sheen of Lavender Cotton. These are only some of the many uses for ground covers in the landscape scheme.

What Is a Ground Cover?

Ground covers are a diverse group of low-growing plants; they may be shrubs, vines, perennials, or annuals. An important part of any garden, ground covers link a house with its surroundings and ensure the success of the design by unifying the other elements in the landscape—trees, shrubs, walkways, patios, and lawns. When chosen carefully and used creatively, these practical plants can add considerable interest to your home setting.

No single ground cover can fill every need, but many choices exist. Some ground covers are evergreen; others are deciduous, losing their leaves in winter. Ground covers with tenacious roots can help prevent erosion of steep banks; others can be used on slopes where mowing grass would be difficult. Many

ground covers thrive in poor soil or areas that bake in the sun
—places where a lawn would not grow well. Ground covers
are a practical and attractive way to break up large expanses
of lawn that would otherwise be of little visual interest.

Types of Ground Covers

Plants that make good ground covers come from every cate-
gory: They may be perennials, biennials, annuals, vines, or
low-growing shrubs.

A perennial is a plant that grows and flowers each year, dies
back to the ground in winter, and grows again the following
spring. (Certain perennials are not winter hardy in every part
of the country; in cold areas, they may be planted in early
spring and grown as annuals.) A biennial is a plant that produces only foliage in its first year of growth; in the second
year, it flowers, sets seed, and dies. Some biennials, if started
early enough, will actually bloom the first year and can be
grown as annuals, too. An annual is a plant that grows, flowers, sets seed, and dies in the same year. Annual ground covers
are particularly useful for temporary landscaping or as a short-
term planting between small, young plants.

The climbing woody perennials that we call vines are effective
as ground covers because they produce long, pliable stems
that conform to the shape of the ground as they creep along.
Many vines also root as they grow, making a dense, tight
cover. Low-growing, spreading shrubs also make excellent
ground covers, especially where the outline of their horizontal
branches can be seen.

Deciduous or Evergreen?

Woody plants may be either evergreen or deciduous. The leaves of deciduous plants dry up and drop in the fall; when temperatures rise in spring, the plants produce a new set of leaves. Evergreens retain some or all of their foliage during the winter dormancy. Most of the time the leaves remain green, but the leaves of some evergreens may turn color in fall. Many evergreens shed some of their older needles or foliage in the spring as new growth appears. Some hardy herbaceous (non-woody) perennials are also evergreen, which increases their value as ground covers.

Whether to use evergreen or deciduous ground covers is largely a matter of personal preference and the requirements of your garden. If you have a large, bare stretch that is unattractive in winter, you will probably want to select an evergreen ground cover. Deciduous ground covers are generally best in areas where snow covers the ground for most of the winter. Under deciduous trees and shrubs, a deciduous ground cover is perfectly acceptable; but a large expanse of hillside may call for winter greenery.

How Ground Covers Spread

A plant's value as a ground cover comes primarily from its horizontal growth habit, which in turn may be the result of one of several characteristics. Many of the low-growing shrubs have branches that extend out to the sides, either close to or on the ground. These wide-spreading branches may or may not root where they touch the ground, depending on the plant. Other ground covers increase by producing suckers, or new stems, at the base of the plant, so that the diameter of the plant gradually increases. Vining plants send out long runners, which generally root as they creep along the ground. Some ground covers spread by rhizomes or stolons, which are stems or roots that spread underground or just at ground level, sending up new erect stems as they grow. The flowers of some ground covers drop seeds that easily self-sow, increasing the planting rapidly.

First Steps

The ground covers that you plant must be able to survive in your garden, whether it is hot or cold, dry or wet. Some ground covers are so rugged that they will grow almost any-where; others have very specific growing needs. Because they prefer full sun, many of the ground covers in this book are excellent choices for problem areas such as steep slopes that bake in the sun all day. Some ground covers will prevent soil erosion; many of these tolerate dry, sandy soil and salt spray, and are especially useful at the seashore. Before selecting ground covers, assess your needs and choose plants that will match those needs and your environmental conditions.

Hardiness

When selecting ground covers, you must opt for those that are winter hardy where you live (unless you are going to be growing ground covers as annuals). Refer to the zone map on pages 106–107. Devised by the U.S. Department of Agriculture, the map divides North America into ten climate "zones," based on average minimum winter temperatures. Find where you live on the map, determine your hardiness zone, and refer to the plant accounts to select plants that are hardy enough for your climate. Keep in mind, however, that the zone boundaries give an approximation of average winter temperatures; any given year could be colder or warmer than average. Altitude, rainfall, and soil type can also affect hardiness.

Additionally, the topography and architectural features of your property can create microclimates that could affect your choice of ground covers. Temperatures are usually lower, for example, on the north side of a house or at the bottom of a hill. If an area is exposed to wind in winter, you will need to choose a hardier plant than you would grow in a protected spot. Areas that receive plenty of sun are usually warmer than those that do not, especially if they are protected from the wind by a fence or other barrier.

Beginners will do best to stick with plants that they know are hardy in their areas. With experience, you can begin to experiment, testing a plant in a small area before you cover large expanses with it.

Light

The ground covers discussed in this book will grow in full sun, meaning six or more hours of direct sun each day. The plants don't need sun from dawn to dusk, although they might be able to tolerate it. In the heat of summer, most plants respond favorably to protection from intense midday sun. Sun-loving plants will also survive if they receive lightly filtered sun all day.

Full sun often goes hand in hand with hot, dry growing conditions. If this describes your garden, there are many ground covers discussed in this book that will grow happily in such spots, under what may seem like adverse conditions.

Garden Soil

Almost every ground cover prefers soil that is well drained. Beyond that, the preference for soil that is dry or moist and rich or poor varies with the plant. Before you decide what to grow, refer to the plant accounts and make sure the ground covers you select will fit your growing conditions.

Rich soil is soil that is high in organic matter. If your soil is not naturally rich, you can improve it by adding organic matter, which will also help to retain moisture and nutrients, provide better drainage, and activate beneficial organisms. Peat moss is the most commonly used source of organic matter, but you can also use leaf mold, dehydrated manure, or compost. If you wish to grow a plant that prefers poor soil, add little or no organic matter when preparing the soil. Average soil usually contains about 25 percent organic matter.

The Importance of pH

The measure of a soil's alkalinity or acidity is known as pH. The pH of soil is important because it affects the ability of plants to take up nutrients through their roots. The pH is measured on a scale of 1 to 14, with 7 being neutral; lower numbers indicate acid soil, higher numbers alkaline soil. Most ground covers prefer a slightly acid to neutral soil with a pH of 5.5 to 7.0. If a plant needs a more acid soil, you can lower the pH by adding sulfur. If you need a more alkaline soil, you can raise the pH by adding limestone. Dolomitic limestone is the best type to use, as it is slow acting, does not burn, and contains magnesium and calcium.

If you are not sure of the pH of your soil, don't guess. Buy a soil test kit at your garden supply store, or have a soil sample tested by your local Cooperative Extension Service or a soil testing lab. If you live in the East or Northwest, your soil is most likely acid; if you live in the Midwest or Southwest, it is probably alkaline.

Fertilizer

Fertilizer contains nitrogen, phosphorus, and potassium in varying quantities. The proportion of each of these elements in commercial fertilizer is expressed as a ratio and clearly marked on the label by a series of three numbers; 5–10–5 fertilizer, for example, contains 5 percent nitrogen, 10 percent phosphate, and 5 percent potash. Other typical proportions are 5–10–10, 10–10–10, and 10–6–4. Most ground covers benefit from the yearly application of one of these complete fertilizers.

Ground covers that are grown primarily for their foliage can be fed any complete fertilizer; fertilizer high in nitrogen (the first number in the series) will promote lush leaf growth. Ground covers grown for their flowers should not be fed high-nitrogen fertilizer, which encourages stem and foliage growth at the expense of flowering. A fertilizer with a 1:2:1 or 1:2:2 ratio is best for these plants.

Getting Started

Before you start to dig a bed for your ground covers, there are several things to do to ensure that your new plants will have a long, healthy life and will be an asset to your garden. The first step is to make a design—a rough sketch or pencilled layout will do—of where you want the plants to go; and then you must prepare the ground for them.

Designing with Ground Covers

We have seen that you should choose your ground covers with a view to their needs for light, soil, and water. You should also consider their purpose in the garden and several other factors, including flower color, foliage, fall color, and berries, whether the plant is deciduous or evergreen, and how it will look in the winter. When using a ground cover to unify a tree or shrub border, it is best to use only one type of plant; otherwise your creation will look disjointed and busy.

In deciding how to lay out your area, envision shapes on the ground. You can use formal, geometric shapes, or less formal, flowing curves. Beds can be created where there are no plants, or between and around existing plants. Sketch the design and make an estimate of how many plants you will need to buy, based on their size and growth habit. (This information is found in the plant accounts.)

Buying Ground Covers

Most ground covers are sold in containers or in flats. When you go shopping, look for healthy, green plants that show signs of growth and have no indication of insects or diseases.

Try to find plants that have been well watered and cared for, and avoid those with roots growing out of the bottom of the pot. Choose plants whose height and size will be in proportion to the overall design.

Preparing the Soil

Because ground covers live for many years in the same spot, it is essential to prepare the soil well before you plant them. If you are preparing a new bed, first remove all grass, weeds, and debris. Next, test the soil to see if it can be worked: Take a handful and squeeze it into a ball. If it remains solid and sticky, it is still too wet; wait a few days and try again. When the soil ball crumbles easily, it is ready. If the soil is dry or dusty, water it several days before preparing it.

Add organic matter as needed to the top of the soil, and use a Rototiller or spade to mix it in to a depth of 18 inches. Complete fertilizer is usually not added at this time, but a source of phosphorus such as superphosphate (0–46–0), added at the rate of 5 pounds per 100 square feet, will ensure good root growth. This is also the time to adjust the pH if necessary. After these amendments are thoroughly mixed into the soil, rake it level and allow it to settle for several days.

Planting Ground Covers

When you have made all your preparations and purchased your plants, you have arrived at the big moment—now you are ready to plant your ground covers.

When to Plant

The timing of planting depends on your climate. In very cold climates, spring planting is preferred because plants then have a long growing season to become established before winter comes. If planted in fall, ground covers may not have enough time to become established before winter and may heave out of the ground. In warmer areas, plants may be added to the garden either in early spring (so they are established before summer's heat comes) or in early fall, about two to three months before the first frost. Ground covers can be planted in summer, but only if you can give them a lot of care.

How to Plant

If you are planting a new bed, lay the plants on the ground in their pots according to your design and move them around until you are satisfied with the arrangement. A staggered row pattern looks best and helps control erosion. If the bed is wide, place a board on it so you do not step directly onto the newly prepared soil and compact it.

Space ground covers according to the type of plant, how fast it grows, how quickly you want to cover the area, and your budget. The more closely you space plants, the more quickly the area will be covered, but the more expensive it will be. As a guide, plan on spacing herbaceous perennials and vining plants 1 foot apart and shrubs 3 feet apart.

Before planting, water both the new plants and the soil. Then dig a hole that is slightly larger than the individual plant's root ball. Remove the plant from its pot by turning the pot upside down and, if necessary, hitting the bottom of the pot to release the root ball. Loosen and spread out any roots that are tightly wound around the plant, and set the plant in the hole so it will be growing at the same level at which it grew in the pot. Gently firm the soil around the roots.

If you are planting large plants, refill the planting hole only halfway with soil, fill the hole with water, let it drain, and then fill the rest of the hole with soil. This will eliminate air pockets and ensure that roots are in direct contact with soil.

After planting, water each plant well, and water again daily until you see signs of new growth. Build a ring of soil around the base of large plants to help them collect water and draw it to the roots until they are well established.

Planting on Slopes

In addition to serving as attractive carpets over bare slopes, ground covers can also help solve erosion problems. Until the plants are well established, however, they may contribute to the problem if they are not properly situated. The degree of slope will determine your planting method. On all slopes, staggered planting will help prevent gullies that form when water runs straight downhill. On gentle slopes of 20 degrees or less, build up the soil on the downhill side of each plant to catch water and to control erosion. On steeper slopes, terraces across the width of the slope, reinforced with boards and stakes, will control runoff. On very steep slopes, retaining walls will be needed.

Choose ground covers with deep roots for use on slopes, since they will hold the soil in place better. Until the plants are established, you can use landscape cloth (a sheet of fabric mulch available at garden centers) to hold the soil in place and prevent weeds from germinating.

Caring for Ground Covers

Like all garden plants, ground covers need day-to-day maintenance to grow at their best. It is a good idea to tour your grounds every day when plants are new and at least weekly thereafter, so you can catch any small problems before they get out of hand.

Watering

Water requirements vary from plant to plant; check the plant descriptions for the specific needs of those in your garden. In general, plants with narrow or needlelike leaves require less water than plants with large leaves. Ground covers with silver or gray foliage tolerate much drier soil than plants with green leaves. A plant that requires average moisture should be watered once a week unless it is very hot or windy. Watch your garden closely and adjust watering as necessary, especially if you see signs of wilting.

Fertilizing

Unless directions are given to the contrary in the plant accounts, most ground covers benefit from the application of a complete fertilizer in early spring to mid-spring, when growth starts. Water the ground well first, apply the fertilizer, and then water again to carry the fertilizer to the roots.

Mulching and Weeding

Mulch is a layer of material, usually organic, placed on the soil to act as insulation, keep the soil at an even temperature, and retard evaporation. Mulch is especially important when you are growing plants in full sun, as it conserves moisture and keeps the ground and the plants' roots cooler. A bonus is that it also helps keep weeds from growing. When your ground covers are newly planted, mulch them until they grow into a thick carpet.

Many different types of mulch are available; the best include bark chips, buckwheat hulls, shredded leaves, and pine needles. Peat moss is not a good mulch, and grass clippings, while readily available, must be dried first and break down too fast. When choosing a mulch, consider availability, cost, durability, and appearance.

Remove weeds as soon as they appear; they compete with the ground covers for food, water, and light. In addition, they are often breeding grounds for insects and diseases. Pull weeds by hand after a rain or a watering; you can weed large areas with a hoe. If you like, try pre-emergent herbicides, which prevent weed seeds from germinating and are safe to use around ground covers; don't use any other type of herbicide.

Pruning and Trimming

Ground covers do not need heavy pruning. The amount required depends more on their appearance than on anything else. Early spring is the best time to prune woody plants, as the new growth will quickly cover any bare stems. Cut out any dead branches or winter-burned growing tips and shape the plants as needed. You can clip back vining ground covers any time they start to overgrow the area. Avoid pruning in late summer or fall because that can encourage new growth, which may not harden off before winter.

Propagation

You can propagate ground covers in a number of ways, depending on the type of plant. Propagating your own plants is an easy and inexpensive way to increase your plantings and to share ground covers with friends and neighbors.

Division

Division is the easiest way to increase perennial and vining ground covers and some shrubby plants. It is best done in early spring, when growth starts, or in late summer, about two months before the first fall frost. To divide plants, dig them up carefully, disturbing their roots as little as possible. Wash the soil off the roots if necessary, to see what you are doing. Pull the plant apart with your hands; some plants have heavy root systems, and you will need to use a spade or trowel. Replant all the resulting divisions before the roots dry out. If you divide plants in late summer, prune the tops back by about half to compensate for the lost roots. If you divide plants in spring, prune the tops only if there is a substantial amount of new growth.

Cuttings

Perennials, vines, and shrubby plants can often be propagated by stem cuttings. This method will yield a larger number of plants than division, but it also requires more care. The best time to take cuttings from most plants is midsummer to late summer, when growth is neither too soft nor too firm. Choose a shoot that is 3 to 6 inches long and has four to six leaves near the top; the shoots of many woody plants root more quickly if you leave a piece of the main stem, known as a heel, at the base of the cutting. Remove any flowers or flower buds and the bottom two to three leaves to expose the nodes from which the new roots will grow. Place the cutting in a pot or flat containing a moistened mixture of peat moss and sand, planting it deep enough that all of the exposed nodes are below the surface of the medium. (Many woody plants will root faster if you dust a rooting hormone onto the cuttings before planting them.) Cover the flat with a clear plastic bag and place the container in good light but not direct sun.

In about a month, check for rooting by gently tugging on one of the leaves. If the cutting comes out, it has not rooted; replace it and test it again in another few weeks. Once the cutting has rooted, place it in its own pot to grow until it is ready to move to a permanent space in the garden.

Layering

Trailing plants and plants with pliable stems can be increased by layering. The best time to layer plants is in spring or early summer. Secure a trailing stem to the ground with a stick or wire and cover the stem with 1 to 2 inches of soil. Keep the soil moist at all times. You can make a series of layers with long stems by weaving them in and out of the soil. To layer a woody plant, cut into the stem partway on the underside and dust the cut with rooting hormone before covering it.

Perennial and vining ground covers may be rooted by fall; woody plants may not root until the next year. As soon as a large root system is formed, you can cut the stem away from the main plant and transfer it to another part of the garden.

Seeds

Most annual and perennial ground covers can be grown from seeds. Some woody plants can be, too, but this is usually a slower and more difficult process. You can sow seeds directly outdoors if they are not too small and if they will grow into large enough plants during the growing season. Fine seeds and seeds of plants that have long growing seasons—especially ground covers being grown as annuals—should be started indoors.

To sow seeds outdoors, first prepare the soil as described above. Sow the seeds according to packet directions, and keep the soil evenly moist until germination occurs. When the plants are 1 to 2 inches high, thin them so that they are about 6 to 8 inches apart. Seeds of perennial ground covers can be started outdoors from early spring through midsummer.

Indoors, sow seeds in clean, sterile flats or other containers using a soilless, pre-moistened growing medium. Place the seed trays in good light but not bright sun, inside a clear plastic bag to keep the humidity high. Once the seeds have germinated, remove the plastic bag and place the container in full sun or under fluorescent lights. Water, preferably from the bottom, to keep the medium evenly moist at all times. When the plants have four to six leaves, move the seedlings to individual pots to make them easier to transplant later on.

Before the new plants can be added to the garden, they must become accustomed to the outdoor environment. This is called "hardening off." A week before planting, place the seedlings outdoors in the shade in a protected spot, and bring them back inside at night. Gradually increase the time outside and the degree of light until planting time.

Fall and Winter Care

In fall, rake leaves out of the ground covers and do a general garden cleanup. Water the ground deeply because plants will survive the winter better if their roots are not dry. Broadleaf evergreens can be sprayed with antidesiccant to help protect them from sun and wind burn. In windy areas, or if you have planted ground covers with marginal winter hardiness, apply winter protection such as evergreen boughs after the ground freezes, and remove it when growth starts in the spring.

A Note on Plant Names

The common, or English, names of plants are often colorful and evocative: Basket-of-Gold, Snow-in-Summer, Lamb's-Ears. But common names vary widely from region to region: Bearberry and Kinnikinick are both names for the same plant. Sometimes, two very different plants may have the same or similar common names, as with Hybrid Rockrose and Rock Rose. And some have no common name at all. But every plant, fortunately, is assigned a scientific, or Latin, name that is distinct and unique to that plant. Scientific names are not necessarily more correct, but they are standard around the world and governed by an international set of rules. Therefore, even though scientific names may at first seem difficult or intimidating, they are in the long run a simple and sure way of distinguishing one plant from another.

A scientific name has two parts. The first is called the generic name; it tells us to which genus (plural, genera) a plant belongs. The second part of the name tells us the species. (A species is a kind of plant or animal that is capable of reproducing with members of its kind but is genetically isolated from others. *Homo sapiens* is a species.) Most genera have many species; *Cotoneaster,* for example, has more than 50. *Cotoneaster dammeri,* Bearberry Cotoneaster, is a species in this book.

Some scientific names have a third part, which may be in italics or written within single quotation marks in roman type. This third part designates a variety or cultivar; some species may have dozens of varieties or cultivars that differ from the species in plant size, plant form, flower size, or flower color. Technically, a variety is a plant that is naturally produced, while a cultivar (short for "cultivated variety") has been created by a plant breeder. For the purposes of the gardener, they may be treated as the same thing. *Aurinia saxitilis* 'Citrina' is one example.

A hybrid is a plant that is the result of a cross between two genera, two species, or two varieties or cultivars. Sometimes hybrids are given a new scientific name, but they are usually indicated by an × within the scientific name: *Caryopteris × clandonensis,* Bluebeard, is a hybrid in this book.

Organization of the Plant Accounts

The plant accounts in this book are arranged alphabetically by scientific name. If you know only the common name of a ground cover, refer to the index and turn to the page given.

Some accounts in the book deal with a garden plant at the genus level—because the genus includes many similar species that can be treated in more or less the same way in the garden. In these accounts, only the genus name is given at the top of the page; the name of the species, cultivar, or hybrid pictured is given within the text.

One Last Word

Now you are ready to choose the sun-loving ground covers that will be best for your garden. Turn to the plant descriptions that follow, make your selections, and then prepare to see your property transformed into a lush carpet of beautifully landscaped color.

Ground Covers for Sun

Woolly Yarrow *(Achillea tomentosa)*

Woolly Yarrow has finely divided, gray-green leaves that are hairy and aromatic. The leaves spread to form a mat 2 inches high and up to 2 feet wide. The basal leaves may be evergreen or semi-evergreen in warmer climates. Tiny, bright yellow flowers bloom in early summer to midsummer in flat-topped, 1-inch clusters on 6- to 10-inch stems. Woolly Yarrow may be used as a ground cover, in the rock garden, or as an edging plant.

GROWING TIPS

Woolly Yarrow is an excellent plant for full, hot sun and sandy, poor, or dry soil with good drainage. To keep the plants neat, cut them back after they have flowered; mow them if plantings become too dense. Woolly Yarrow has a tendency to be weedy and may need thinning or dividing every year. New plants can be propagated from seeds or stem cuttings.

Pussytoes *(Antennaria dioica)*

Pussytoes has rosettes of hairy, 1- to 1½-inch, basal leaves that spread to cover large areas. The leaves are dark green on the upper surfaces and white and woolly on the undersides. The tubular, ¼-inch white flowers are tipped in pink and look like cats' feet. They bloom in loose clusters in early summer atop 4- to 12-inch stems. The variety *rosea,* pictured, has pink flowers. The blooms make pretty cut flowers and also dry very well.

GROWING TIPS

Pussytoes is a useful ground cover in dry, open spaces with poor soil. It likes full sun and sandy, well-drained soil. Pussytoes self-sows easily and can become weedy. Cut the flowers off before they drop their seeds to help prevent this. The plants can be divided when they become crowded.

Rock Cress *(Arabis)*

Rock Cress, *A. procurrens* (pictured), has hairy, bright green leaves clothing its short, creeping stems. Masses of single white flowers bloom in mid-spring on 12-inch stalks. The flowers are ¼ inch across and have 4 petals. Wall Cress, *A. caucasica,* has 4- to 6-inch-high mats of gray-green leaves. Fragrant, ½-inch flowers bloom in loose clusters on 12-inch stems. The blooms, which may be single or double, are white or pink. Both plants are excellent in rock gardens or cascading from the top of a wall.

GROWING TIPS

Rock Cress grows best in full sun. It prefers warm, dry, sandy soil and must have excellent drainage. It will not grow well in areas with hot, humid summers. Wall Cress, by contrast, does better in rich soil and will tolerate either dry or moist growing conditions. Both *Arabis* species can be increased by division, from cuttings, or from seeds.

Bearberry *(Arctostaphylos uva-ursi)*

Zone 3

A shrubby, evergreen ground cover, Bearberry, also known as Kinnikinick, has glossy dark green leaves that turn bronze in the winter. The leaves are smooth and oblong, growing 1 inch long. The reddish or brown branches are prostrate and grow crookedly, rooting as they spread along the ground. The plants grow 2–8 inches high and spread to more than 12 feet across. Tiny, pink, bell-shaped flowers appear in spring. They are followed by long-lasting, ¼-inch red berries.

Bearberry is most attractive covering an area over and around rocks, where the outline of its branches can be seen.

GROWING TIPS

Plant Bearberry in full sun and dry, sandy, acid soil that has excellent drainage. Bearberry will not grow well in areas where freezing temperatures do not occur in winter. Propagate Bearberry plants from stem cuttings, by layering, or from seeds.

African Daisy *(Arctotis)*

African Daisy hybrids, perennial in frost-free climates, can be grown as an annual ground cover in other areas. Deeply cut or toothed leaves grow at the base of the plant. The flowers are daisylike and bloom on leafless, 10- to 12-inch stems. Blooms may be white, yellow, pink, bronze, red, purple, orange, or brown.

GROWING TIPS

African Daisies prefer full sun and dry, sandy soil. Do not over-water them, and fertilize little if at all. They prefer cool nights and are best grown in spring or fall where summers are hot. To promote flowering and to keep plants neat, remove flowers as soon as they fade. African Daisies are best propagated from seeds or stem cuttings.

Mountain Sandwort *(Arenaria montana)*

An evergreen, Mountain Sandwort forms 2- to 4-inch-high mats of narrow, grasslike, trailing foliage. The leaves are soft, glossy, and gray-green, growing 1 inch long. Flowers bloom in profusion in late spring or early summer. They are 1 inch across, white with yellow centers, and have 5 rounded petals. Because it is so low growing and will withstand light foot traffic, Mountain Sandwort is often used between stepping stones and also in rock gardens.

GROWING TIPS

Mountain Sandwort prefers a spot in full sun, especially where summers are cool. It grows in average soil but prefers soil that is moist, slightly acid, and well drained. Mountain Sandwort plants can be divided or propagated from cuttings, but they are best grown from seeds.

Common Thrift *(Armeria maritima)*

An evergreen, Common Thrift has grassy, bluish-green leaves that grow in rosettes at the base of the plant. In late spring and summer, dense, globe-shaped clusters of pink, white, rose, or purple flowers appear. The stiff, leafless flowering stems grow 6–12 inches high. Common Thrift can be used along walkways, between stepping stones, in borders, or in a seashore garden.

GROWING TIPS

Plant Common Thrift in full sun and sandy, loamy soil that is well drained. If the soil is too moist or too fertile, the mat of leaves will decay in the center and flowering will decrease. Propagate Common Thrift by dividing mature plants in spring or fall.

Beach Wormwood (*Artemisia stellerana*)

Beach Wormwood is a bushy, 2-foot-high, aromatic species, grown primarily for its foliage. It is sometimes called Dusty Miller (as are several other plants). Its leaves are white, felty, and deeply lobed; it has tiny, inconspicuous, yellow flowers in late summer or fall. Beach Wormwood is excellent as an edging, a border plant, a buffer between strong colors, and a dense, shrubby ground cover. It is very tolerant of salt air.

GROWING TIPS

Beach Wormwood grows best in full sun and soil that is dry, sandy, and very well drained, especially during the winter. In areas with poor drainage, Beach Wormwood is best grown as an annual. You can shear plants in midsummer to encourage dense growth, although this will prevent flowering. Beach Wormwood plants are propagated from cuttings or by division.

Basket-of-Gold *(Aurinia saxitilis)*

The dense masses of blooms that give Basket-of-Gold its name are so heavy that the flowering stems usually cannot stand erect. For this reason, Basket-of-Gold is especially effective cascading over rocks and walls. Clumps of oblong, gray-green leaves grow at the base of the plants. In mid-spring, the single, ⅛-inch-wide golden-yellow flowers bloom on 6- to 12-inch stems. 'Citrina', pictured, has paler yellow flowers than the species. Basket-of-Gold was formerly known as *Alyssum saxatile* and is sometimes still sold by that name.

GROWING TIPS

Plant Basket-of-Gold in full sun, in any garden soil with good drainage. Fertilize the plants very lightly to keep them from becoming scraggly. After the plants have flowered, shear them back to keep them compact. Basket-of-Gold does not grow well in hot, humid climates. It develops a long taproot and is difficult to transplant. New plants can be grown from seeds.

Dwarf Coyote Brush *(Baccharis pilularis)*

Dwarf Coyote Brush is an evergreen shrub that grows 1–2 feet tall and spreads by trailing branches to form a mat 6 feet wide. It has thick, fleshy, bright green leaves that are toothed and grow to 1 inch long. Tiny, off-white, tubular flowers bloom in the fall in small, dense heads. There are separate male and female plants; the female plants form fluffy, messy seed heads after flowering. 'Twin Peaks' is an all-male variety.

GROWING TIPS

Dwarf Coyote Brush tolerates a wide range of growing conditions, from full sun to full shade and very wet to very dry soil, but it grows best in full sun and rich, moist soil. In early spring, prune old branches to the ground. Propagate new plants from cuttings or from seeds. Dwarf Coyote Brush has a strong root system and is useful for holding banks, slopes, and sand dunes in place.

Warty Barberry *(Berberis verruculosa)*

A 3-foot-tall evergreen shrub, Warty Barberry has spiny, leathery, 1-inch leaves that are glossy and dark green on the upper surfaces and white on the undersides. The leaves grow in clusters at the ends of short spurs and turn bronze in the fall. Yellow flowers bloom in the spring; the berries that follow are purple to black and are covered with whitish powder. The plant is named for its warty branches, which have long thorns.

GROWING TIPS

Warty Barberry prefers full sun and moist, well-drained soil. It grows best in areas with freezing temperatures in winter. Once established, it does not transplant well. New plants can be grown from cuttings. Because of its thorns, Warty Barberry is a good barrier plant.

Spike-Heath *(Bruckenthalia spiculifolia)*

Spike-Heath, like other members of the heath family, has small, needlelike leaves and bell-shaped flowers. This shrubby evergreen has creeping branches that root as they grow along the ground and bear upright stems that are densely covered with foliage. Spike-Heath plants grow 6–10 inches high and spread to 18 inches across. The flowers, which are ¼ inch long and have 4 deep lobes, bloom in short, ¾-inch spikes during the summer.

GROWING TIPS

Spike-Heath grows best in full sun and rich, slightly acid, well-drained soil. To propagate Spike-Heath, divide older plants or grow new ones from seeds. Spike-Heath is a good ground cover on banks or slopes. Because of its resemblance to heather and heath, it is a good substitute for those plants where they do not grow well.

Heather *(Calluna vulgaris)*

Heather is a shrubby, evergreen ground cover that forms a spreading mound 1½ feet tall and 2–4 feet across. The branches are covered with fine, scalelike, bright to dark green leaves. Some varieties have foliage that turns red or orange in the fall and winter. The nodding, bell-shaped flowers bloom in 10-inch spikes in late summer and fall. The tiny blooms, which may be single or double, are white, pink, or lavender. 'J. H. Hamilton', pictured, is a late-flowering variety with double pink flowers.

GROWING TIPS

Heather grows best in full sun and poor, moist soil that is acidic and well drained. It grows well at the seashore. The roots are shallow; be careful when you weed not to damage or disturb them. Apply a mulch in summer to keep the soil cool and moist. Give heather protection from very cold temperatures and winter winds. In early spring, prune the plants back. Propagate new plants from cuttings taken in summer.

Carpathian Harebell *(Campanula carpatica)* Zone 4

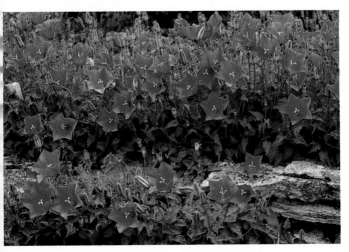

Carpathian Harebell has round, serrated leaves that grow densely at the base of the plant. Two-inch, bell-shaped flowers in shades of blue, purple, or white appear during the spring and summer. They face upward on this species of bellflower; on others the blooms are nodding. Carpathian Harebell is a long-flowering plant good for edging. It grows 6–12 inches high.

Growing Tips
Plant Carpathian Harebell in full sun or partial shade; in very hot climates, protect it from afternoon sun. It will grow in any garden soil but it prefers fertile, moist soil with good drainage. Start new Carpathian Harebell plants from cuttings, by division, or from seeds.

Bellflower *(Campanula elatines garganica)*

This sprawling bellflower grows 6–10 inches high. Small, hairy leaves that grow at the base of the plant form a dense ground cover. Bellflower starts to bloom in the spring and blooms off and on all summer. The ½-inch, blue flowers are star shaped and bloom in sprays. Bellflower is useful as a ground cover, in rock gardens, or on top of walls.

GROWING TIPS

Bellflower grows well in either full sun or light shade; it prefers some shade in very hot climates. It grows best in rich, moist, well-drained soil, but it will tolerate dry soil as well. Cut the plants back after they have bloomed to keep them neat. Propagate new plants by division, from cuttings, or from seeds.

Bluebeard *(Caryopteris × clandonensis)*

Bluebeard, also called Blue Spirea, is a mounded, deciduous shrub that grows 2 feet high. The 3-inch-long leaves are lance shaped and toothed. Small, blue flowers with 5 lobes bloom in profuse clusters during the late summer. Two popular cultivars are 'Blue Mist' and 'Kew Blue', pictured. Plant Bluebeard with pink Bumald Spirea *(Spiraea × bumalda)* for a pretty color combination in the late summer garden.

GROWING TIPS
Bluebeard grows best in full sun and slightly rich, well-drained garden soil. Keep the soil evenly moist at all times. Provide winter protection for Bluebeard in the colder limits of its hardiness. In winter or very early spring, cut the stems almost to the ground to keep the plants compact. Propagate new plants from stem cuttings.

Point Reyes Ceanothus *(Ceanothus gloriosus)*   Zone 7

GROWING TIPS

Point Reyes Ceanothus belongs to a genus of shrubs sometimes called wild lilacs. Its flowers are light blue to lavender and bloom in cone-shaped clusters in spring. This is a rapid-growing, very dense species that reaches 4–18 inches in height and spreads 5–10 feet across. The leathery, dark green leaves are toothed and grow 1½ inches long; they last well into the winter before they fall.

Plant Point Reyes Ceanothus in full sun. It prefers light, well-drained soil. It does not grow well where summers are hot but does grow well in coastal climates. Start new plants from cuttings, by layering, or from seeds.

Snow-in-Summer *(Cerastium tomentosum)*

Snow-in-Summer is a fast-growing plant with white, woolly foliage. The pointed, 1-inch leaves form a mat 6 inches high and 1½–2 feet across. Showy, white, ½-inch flowers with notched petals bloom in late spring and summer. Snow-in-Summer is a popular plant in the rock garden or low border.

GROWING TIPS

Like most plants with white or gray foliage, Snow-in-Summer grows best in full sun and poor, dry, well-drained soil. It will even grow in pure sand. Snow-in-Summer can be quite weedy; cut back the plants as soon as the flowers fade to keep them compact and to prevent self-seeding. Dense plantings can be mowed in early spring when growth starts. Propagate new plants by division, from stem cuttings, or from seeds.

Leadwort *(Ceratostigma plumbaginoides)*

Leadwort grows 6–12 inches tall and can quickly cover an area several feet across. The pointed, oval leaves are 3½ inches long and hairy along the margins. They turn red in the fall; in warm climates, they are evergreen. Tubular, blue flowers bloom in clusters in late summer and fall. The flowers are ½–1 inch across and have 5 lobes.

GROWING TIPS

Leadwort grows best in full sun and fertile, well-drained soil, but it will tolerate poor, dry soil and some shade. It also tolerates high summer heat. Leadwort emerges late in the spring, so take care not to damage dormant plants. Propagate from cuttings or by division in spring. Leadwort needs winter protection in the northern limits of its hardiness.

Roman Chamomile *(Chamaemelum nobile)*

Roman Chamomile has gray-green, finely cut foliage that grows 6 inches high and 1½ feet across. The aromatic leaves are 2 inches long. Fragrant, ½- to 1-inch flowers bloom in late summer. The flowers are usually daisylike with yellow centers and white petals, but sometimes they bloom without petals. Roman Chamomile tolerates light foot traffic and can be used between stepping stones. It was formerly called *Anthemis nobilis.*

GROWING TIPS

Roman Chamomile grows best in full sun and poor, sandy, well-drained soil. Water new plants heavily; mature plants will tolerate both moist soil and drought. Roman Chamomile readily self-seeds; keep it in check by removing the flower heads before they drop their seeds. It can also be propagated from cuttings or by division. Mow dense plantings in early spring to encourage compact growth.

Hybrid Rockrose *(Cistus × pulverulentus)*

This evergreen or semievergreen ground cover grows 2 feet tall and has soft, hairy, oval leaves. The rose-red flowers, which are 1 inch across and have 5 petals, bloom in summer. They look something like single roses. Hybrid Rockroses are quite fire retardant and are popular as ground covers and border plants in the dry areas of the West. They are also used in rock gardens.

Growing Tips

Hybrid Rockroses must have full sun and dry, slightly alkaline, well-drained soil. They will tolerate drought but do not tolerate cold, wet winters. Hybrid Rockrose plants are difficult to transplant. Grow new plants from seeds or stem cuttings.

Crown Vetch (*Coronilla varia*)

Crown Vetch is a fast-growing, deciduous, creeping ground cover that is much used on slopes that are difficult to mow and that need erosion control. The plants grow 1½–2 feet tall and up to 4 feet wide. The soft green leaves are feathery, and the pink and white flowers resemble those of the Sweet Pea. The blooms are ½ inch long, appearing in clusters in summer. 'Penngift', a popular variety, grows 1–1½ feet high and is very drought resistant.

GROWING TIPS
Crown Vetch likes full sun and dry, well-drained soil. It should not be fertilized. Mow it once in early spring to encourage compact growth. Crown Vetch can be propagated from seeds and from root divisions. Its seeds are often sold with seeds of annual ryegrass, which anchors the Crown Vetch in place until it becomes established.

Bearberry Cotoneaster (*Cotoneaster dammeri*) Zone 5

earberry Cotoneaster is an ever-green shrub that grows 1 foot high and has graceful, trailing branches that spread to 6 feet across. The branches root at the stem joints. The inch-long, oval leaves are shiny and dark green, with pale green undersides; they turn reddish purple in the fall. Small white flowers bloom in mid-spring; attrac-tive red berries are produced in the fall. The variety 'Skogsholm', pictured here, blooms more pro-fusely than the species.

GROWING TIPS

Bearberry Cotoneaster prefers a spot in full sun but will tolerate some shade. It likes a well-drained soil that is neutral to slightly acid. Once established, Bearberry Cotoneaster will tolerate drought and wind. Large plants are difficult to trans-plant. New plants can be grown from cuttings or by layering.

Rock, or Rockspray, Cotoneaster is a deciduous shrub (in zones 8–10 it may be evergreen) that grows 2–3 feet high. The branches are stiff and spread out like a fan. This cotoneaster is most effective planted between rocks where the outline of its branches can be seen. The round, ½-inch-long leaves are shiny and dark green; they turn orange-red in fall. Tiny white or pink flowers bloom in mid-spring; small red berries form along the branches in the fall.

GROWING TIPS

Rock Cotoneaster prefers a sunny location but will tolerate some afternoon shade. It grows best in well-drained soil that is neutral to slightly acid. Cotoneasters are relatively easy to grow and require pruning only when they need to be shaped. Unfortunately, they are subject to fire blight, inchworms, and, in dry summers, to lace bugs and spider mites. Propagate new plants from cuttings or by layering.

Irish Heath *(Daboecia cantabrica)*

Irish Heath is a low-growing, shrubby evergreen that resembles the true heaths *(Erica)*. The ½-inch, needlelike leaves are dark green and glossy on top and white on the undersides. Erect, spreading branches grow slowly to 1½–2 feet high. Nodding, bell-shaped flowers bloom in clusters at the ends of the branches in late summer and fall. The blooms are white, pink, or purple. Irish Heath is sometimes sold as *D. polifolia* or *Menziesia polifolia.*

GROWING TIPS

Irish Heath grows best in full sun and light, moist, acid soil that has excellent drainage. Apply winter protection in the northern limits of Irish Heath's hardiness. Propagate new plants from cuttings, by layering, or from seeds.

Rose Daphne *(Daphne cneorum)*

Rose Daphne has richly fragrant flowers, which bloom in 1½-inch clusters in mid-spring, covering the tops of the plants. The bell-shaped flowers are white or pink and have 4 petals. The branches of these shrubby evergreens are covered with narrow, dark green leaves with gray-green undersides; one variety has leaves with white margins. Rose Daphne plants grow 1 foot tall and spread to 2–3 feet across. The leathery, fleshy berries, as well as the bark and leaves, are toxic. The variety 'Eximea' is pictured here.

GROWING TIPS

Rose Daphne grows best in full sun or light shade and loose, fertile soil; it must have excellent drainage. Protect it from afternoon sun and be careful not to over-water it. The roots are shallow; keep them cool with a mulch and take care not to damage them when you weed. Rose Daphne needs protection from freezing temperatures and winter sun and wind. Propagate new plants from cuttings, by layering, or from seeds.

Cheddar Pink *(Dianthus gratianopolitanus)* Zone 5

Cheddar Pink grows 6–8 inches tall and spreads to form an evergreen mat 12–15 inches across. The ½- to ¾-inch flowers, which are called "pinks" because the petals look like they were cut with pinking shears, may be pink, red, or white. They are single, have 5 petals, and bloom in summer. The foliage is gray-green, narrow, and grassy, and has swollen joints. Cheddar Pink is a good choice for rock gardens or to carpet the ground in a small area.

GROWING TIPS

Plant Cheddar Pinks in full sun or light shade in cool, neutral to alkaline soil that has good drainage. After the flowers have faded, shear back the plants to keep them compact. New plants can be grown from cuttings, by division, or from seeds.

Mock Strawberry *(Duchesnea indica)*

Mock Strawberry resembles, and is related to, the true strawberry. Mock Strawberry plants grow quickly to 2–3 inches high and spread by runners to 1½–2 feet across. The oval, 3-part leaves are dark green and toothed and have silky hairs on the undersides. They do not fall from the plant until well into the winter. Single, 5-petaled, yellow flowers with prominent stamens bloom in the summer. A red, strawberrylike fruit forms in late summer; it is edible but has little flavor.

GROWING TIPS

Plant Mock Strawberry in full sun in any garden soil. It grows best in rich, moist soil but tolerates poor soil and drought. Use Mock Strawberry in large areas; it is a fast grower and can be invasive. Propagate new plants from seeds or by rooting the plantlets that form at the ends of the runners.

Spring Heath *(Erica carnea)*

Spring Heath is a shrubby evergreen with small, shiny, needle-like leaves that are held closely to the branches. The leaves are dark green; in some varieties, they are red or bronze. The bell-shaped flowers, which are white, pink, rose, red, or purple, bloom in nodding clusters in early spring. Spring Heath plants grow 6–18 inches tall and spread 1½–3 feet across. 'Springwood Pink' is pictured.

GROWING TIPS

Spring Heath grows best in full sun and sandy, rich, well-drained soil. Keep the soil evenly moist during the growing period. The roots are shallow; keep them cool and moist with a mulch and be careful not to disturb them when you weed. Spring Heath grows best in high humidity; it needs protection from drying winds. After Spring Heath has flowered, shear the plants back to keep them compact. Propagate new plants from cuttings, by division, or by layering.

Woolly Eriophyllum (*Eriophyllum lanatum*) Zone 5

Woolly Eriophyllum (it is sometimes called Woolly Sunflower because its daisylike blooms resemble those of the sunflower) has woolly, greenish-white foliage. The 1-inch flowers of Woolly Eriophyllum, which are golden yellow and single, bloom from spring into summer. The stems are weak and are covered with crinkled leaves. Woolly Eriophyllum plants grow to 1–2 feet high and wide.

GROWING TIPS

Woolly Eriophyllum must have a spot in full sun and sandy, dry, well-drained soil. Be sure you plant the crown above the level of the soil or it will rot. Woolly Eriophyllum will not grow well where soil is wet or poorly drained during the winter; it grows better on the West Coast than it does in the East. Grow new plants from seeds or by dividing established plants in the spring.

Myrtle Euphorbia *(Euphorbia myrsinites)*

Myrtle Euphorbia is a succulent plant grown for its numerous, fleshy, blue-green leaves. It flowers in the spring; the blooms are small and greenish with chartreuse bracts, but they are not especially attractive. Myrtle Euphorbia plants grow 3–6 inches high and sprawl by long stems to cover an area 1–1½ feet across. Because of its growth habit, it does well in raised beds and rock gardens and on top of rock walls.

GROWING TIPS

Myrtle Euphorbia grows best in full sun and dry, poor, sandy soil. It will not grow well in soil that is poorly drained during the winter. The plants release a milky sap when they are broken that may cause a skin rash, so handle them carefully. Grow new plants from cuttings or by dividing established plants.

Bronx Greenstem Forsythia

(*Forsythia viridissima* 'Bronxensis') Zone 5

Bronx Greenstem Forsythia was so named because it was developed at the New York Botanical Garden in the Bronx. A very low shrub used as a ground cover, it grows only 12–18 inches high and spreads to 3 feet wide. The pointed, oblong leaves are toothed and 1–1½ inches long. Greenish-yellow flowers, in clusters of up to 3 blooms, appear in spring. Bronx Greenstem is not as showy in flower as the large forsythias but it has more blooms than other dwarf forms.

GROWING TIPS

Bronx Greenstem Forsythia will grow in full sun or partial shade in average, well-drained garden soil. The plants will survive cold winters, but flower buds can be destroyed by very cold temperatures. The shrubs are tolerant of air pollution and city conditions. Trim forsythia after it has flowered if necessary. Other forsythias are propagated from stem cuttings; cuttings from this cultivar are difficult to root but well worth the effort.

Beach Strawberry (*Fragaria chiloensis*)

Beach Strawberry, or Sand Strawberry, is a rapid-growing plant that reaches 6–8 inches high and spreads by runners to 1½–2 feet across. It has oval, 3-part leaves that are dark green and glossy and 1–2 inches long. The undersides of the leaves are pale bluish white. White flowers with prominent yellow stamens bloom in late spring. They are 1 inch across and have 6 petals. Strawberries are formed after the flowers.

GROWING TIPS

Beach Strawberry likes full sun and sandy, slightly acid, well-drained soil. It can be invasive, but you can control it by removing the runners and the plantlets that usually form at their ends after the fruit has set. To propagate new plants, grow them from seeds or root the plantlets. Beach Strawberries grow very well at the seashore and can quickly cover large areas.

Salal *(Gaultheria shallon)*

The ultimate size and shape of Salal depends on its growing conditions. In full sun and poor soil, it grows 1½ feet high and makes a low, dense, shrubby ground cover. In shade and moist soil, the plants grow erect to 3 feet high and do not spread as much. Salal's dark green, leathery leaves are evergreen. They are round to oval and grow 4 inches long. Tiny, bell-shaped flowers, either pink or white, bloom in late spring in clusters at the ends of the branches. Edible, purplish-black berries form in the fall.

Growing Tips

To grow Salal as a ground cover, plant it in full sun in poor, acid, well-drained soil. Plants grow slowly from seeds; they are more easily propagated from cuttings.

Broom *(Genista pilosa)*

This deciduous, fast-growing, shrubby plant is one of several plants known commonly as broom. It has ascending, arching branches that grow 4–20 inches high; the plants spread by rooting stems and reach 3–6 feet across. The divided, oblong foliage is ¼–½ inch long and gray-green. These deciduous plants look evergreen because the stems remain green all winter. Yellow flowers, which resemble those of the Sweet Pea, bloom in clusters in late spring or early summer.

GROWING TIPS

Broom grows best in full sun and dry, well-drained soil. Do not fertilize the plants. Broom does not transplant well. New plants can be propagated by layering, from cuttings, or from seeds.

This plant is very different from the annual garden geranium, which is another genus. Pyrenean Cranesbill grows 18 inches high and 2 feet wide. It has deeply cut foliage and 1-inch, rose-pink flowers. In cool areas, the flowers bloom all summer; in hot climates, they appear in late spring and early summer. 'A.T. Johnson', pictured here, grows 12 inches high and has light pink flowers; 'Wargrave Pink' has salmon-pink flowers.

GROWING TIPS

Grow Pyrenean Cranesbill in full sun or light shade; protect it from hot afternoon sun. It grows best in moderately rich soil that is moist and well drained. Divide cranesbill plants in the spring or fall. The named varieties can be propagated from cuttings; the species can be grown from cuttings or seeds.

Creeping Baby's-Breath *(Gypsophila repens)*

Creeping Baby's-Breath grows 6 inches high and spreads to 2 feet across. The smooth, grasslike, blue-green leaves have swollen joints. The ¼-inch flowers bloom in large, delicate clusters in early summer. The blooms are usually white; in the variety 'Rosea', pictured, they are pink. Creeping Baby's-Breath makes a good ground cover or filler plant in a mixed border.

GROWING TIPS

Creeping Baby's-Breath likes a spot in full sun and neutral, well-drained soil that is not too rich. Plant it on slopes, along walkways, or cascading over rocks; once you have given it a permanent home, do not try to move it, as it does not transplant well. Propagate new plants from seeds, from stem cuttings, or by division.

Rock Rose is a creeping, woody plant with rooting branches; t grows 6–12 inches high and up o 3 feet across. The narrow, pointed, hairy leaves may be dark green, gray-green, or silvery. Single, 5-petaled flowers, 1–2 inches across, bloom in clusters in late spring and early summer. They look like small, single roses and have a texture like crepe paper. Each lasts only a day, but plants will bloom for several months. The flower color depends on the variety; 'Raspberry Ripple' is seen here.

GROWING TIPS

Grow Rock Rose in full sun in sandy, neutral to alkaline soil that is either dry or moist and has excellent drainage. Prune the plants after they have flowered to keep them compact and to encourage a second bloom. Protect Rock Rose from winter winds and apply a winter mulch in the northern limits of its hardiness. Rock Rose does not like to be transplanted. Propagate new plants from cuttings or seeds.

Rupturewort *(Herniaria glabra)*

Zone 6

Rupturewort is a short-lived plant that grows 3 inches high and spreads to several feet across by rooting stems. The stems have swollen joints and are densely covered with ¼-inch, oblong leaves. The smooth, bright green leaves turn bronze to red in the fall. Rupturewort is grown for its foliage; its flowers are inconspicuous. Rupturewort is deciduous in zones 6–7 and evergreen in zones 8–10.

Growing Tips

Plant Rupturewort in full sun or light shade in average garden soil that is well drained and slightly fertile. Rupturewort tolerates light foot traffic and can be planted between stepping stones. New plants can be propagated by division or from seeds.

Aaronsbeard St. Johnswort

(Hypericum calycinum)

Zone 5

Aaronsbeard St. Johnswort is a shrubby evergreen that grows 1 foot high and spreads to 2 feet across. The shiny, 3- to 4-inch-long leaves are light to medium green with silvery undersides. The flowers, which bloom all summer, are 2–3 inches across and cup shaped. They are golden yellow and have prominent stamens. Aaronsbeard grows well in large rock gardens and on banks where erosion control is needed.

GROWING TIPS

Plant Aaronsbeard in full sun or partial shade in average or sandy, well-drained garden soil. It grows best in moist soil but will tolerate drought. Fertilize Aaronsbeard very lightly if at all. Give it winter protection in zone 5. Shear the plants back in early spring before growth starts to keep them compact. New plants can be started from cuttings, by division, by layering, or from seeds.

Perennial Candytuft *(Iberis sempervirens)*   Zone 5

Perennial Candytuft is a pretty, mounded plant that is nearly smothered by 1½-inch clusters of white, 4-petaled flowers in mid-spring. The plants grow 9–12 inches high and spread to 18–36 inches across. The dark green leaves, which are evergreen, are narrow and 1½ inches long. 'Autumn Snow', which grows 9 inches high and 3 feet wide, has a second bloom in the fall. 'Snowflake' is a large-flowered variety.

GROWING TIPS

Plant Perennial Candytuft in full sun or partial shade in any well-drained garden soil. It will grow in dry conditions but blooms more when grown in moist soil. After candytuft flowers, shear the plant to keep it compact. Protect Perennial Candytuft from winter winds and mulch it lightly over winter to prevent the evergreen leaves from turning brown. Grow new plants from cuttings, by layering, or from seeds.

Japanese Holly *(Ilex crenata)*

Japanese Holly is an evergreen shrub with smooth, shiny, dark green foliage. The leaves are oblong and grow up to 1 inch long. The cultivar 'Helleri' (pictured), which grows 1–3 feet tall and spreads to 3–6 feet wide, has a flat or mounded top. Its foliage is dull green and ½ inch long. 'Repandens' grows 8–36 inches high and 3–4 feet wide. Both species and cultivars have white flowers and black berries, neither of which is showy.

GROWING TIPS

Japanese Holly grows in full sun or partial shade; its growth is more compact in full sun. It prefers rich, slightly acid soil that is moist and well drained. Japanese Holly will not grow well in areas where freezing temperatures do not occur in winter or where summers are hot and dry. It needs protection from winter sun and wind. Propagate plants from cuttings or seeds. Japanese Holly can be pruned into shapes and is a good choice for a formal garden.

Shore Juniper (*Juniperus conferta*)

Shore Juniper is a coniferous ever-green with tufts of soft, pointed, needlelike leaves that are light green when new and later change to blue-green. Shore Juniper grows 1–1½ feet high and spreads 6–8 feet across. Female plants produce small, round, gray to black berries that are used to flavor gin. 'Blue Pacific' is a handsome cultivar with blue foliage.

GROWING TIPS

Shore Juniper will grow best in full sun and loamy, well-drained soil that is neutral to acidic. Be careful not to over-water it. In spring, trim back any plants that need shaping. Propagate Shore Juniper from cuttings or seeds or by layering or grafting. Junipers are a good choice for seashore gardens; they tolerate sandy soil and salt spray.

Japanese Juniper *(Juniperus procumbens)*

A coniferous evergreen, Japanese Juniper has tufts of spiny-tipped, needlelike leaves that are blue-green with paler undersides and a green midrib. The plants have ascending branches and grow 1–2½ feet high and 10–15 feet wide. The dwarf variety 'Nana', shown here, is similar to the species in appearance but grows to only half the size.

GROWING TIPS
Plant Japanese Juniper in full sun in loamy, acid to neutral soil that is well drained. Do not give junipers too much water. Prune, trim, or shape the plants in spring. Propagate from cuttings or seeds or by layering or grafting. Low-growing junipers can be used to cover flat expanses, on slopes, along walkways, and in the front of foundation plantings and shrub borders.

Weeping Lantana *(Lantana montevidensis)* Zone 9

A tender perennial, Weeping Lantana can be grown as an annual where it is not hardy. The plants are shrubby and grow 1–1½ feet high and 3–6 feet wide. Small, tubular flowers that change color as they age bloom in dense, rounded clusters in summer. The blooms are yellow, orange, pink, red, lavender, and white; a cluster may have blooms of several colors. The rough, oval leaves are coarsely toothed and 1 inch long. They are dark green, often turning purple in the winter, and have a sharp odor when crushed.

GROWING TIPS

Weeping Lantana must be grown in full sun. It tolerates any well-drained garden soil but grows best where soil is poor, dry, and warm. Do not fertilize Weeping Lantana or you will have lush foliage but few flowers. Prune it in early spring to encourage new growth. It is a good plant to use where erosion control is needed and on windy sites. Propagate plants from cuttings or seeds.

English Lavender *(Lavandula angustifolia)* Zone 5

English Lavender is a mounded plant with fragrant, gray-green foliage that is narrow and felty. During the summer, narrow spikes of tiny lavender flowers bloom on 18- to 24-inch stems. Popular varieties include 'Hidcote' and 'Munstead'. Use English Lavender as a ground cover, a low hedge, or a border plant.

GROWING TIPS

English Lavender grows best in dry, sandy, alkaline soil with excellent drainage, especially in winter. Fertile soil reduces both the fragrance and the hardiness of the plants. After English Lavender plants have flowered, cut them back to keep them compact. Divide the plants when they become crowded; new plants can be grown from seeds. English Lavender needs winter protection in the colder limits of its hardiness.

Sand Myrtle *(Leiophyllum buxifolium)* Zone 6

Sand Myrtle is a neat, compact, evergreen shrub that grows in a mounded shape up to 2 feet tall and 3 feet across. The plants have upright branches covered with shiny, oval, ½-inch leaves that turn bronze in the fall. Small, star-shaped flowers with prominent stamens bloom in 1-inch clusters in late spring. The flowers are pink in the bud but white when they open. The variety *prostratum*, Allegheny Sand Myrtle, pictured here, grows only 4 inches high.

GROWING TIPS

Sand Myrtle prefers full sun and moist, rich, acid soil that is well drained. Sand Myrtle and Allegheny Sand Myrtle are useful in rock gardens, as low edging plants, and in seashore gardens. Propagate new plants from cuttings or by layering.

Siberian Carpet Cypress *(Microbiota decussata)* Zone 3

Sometimes called Russian Cypress, this flat-topped evergreen shrub grows 1½–2 feet tall and spreads 4–15 feet across. The branches, which arch in a fanlike manner, bear feathery, scaly leaves that are bright green and turn copper in the fall. The small, berrylike cones have brown scales covering a glossy nut. Siberian Carpet Cypress makes a graceful ground cover in open spaces, on slopes, and near trees and shrubs.

GROWING TIPS
Siberian Carpet Cypress grows equally well in full sun or shade. Plant it in average, well-drained garden soil. Once it is established, it will tolerate drought. Propagate Siberian Carpet Cypress from cuttings or by layering.

Heavenly Bamboo
(*Nandina domestica* 'Harbor Dwarf')

This evergreen shrub is not a true bamboo, but its canelike stems and compound leaves resemble those of bamboo. Each leaf has 2–3 pointed, 2-inch leaflets that are light green and turn red or bronze in the fall. Loose, erect clusters of white flowers bloom in late spring and early summer. In fall, red, ¼-inch berries form in large clusters that last through the winter. 'Harbor Dwarf', which grows 1½–2 feet tall, spreads by underground runners to form a good ground cover.

GROWING TIPS

Heavenly Bamboo displays its brightest fall color and showiest berries when grown in full sun. It prefers soil that is moist and well drained. For heavy berry production, you must put several plants close together. Propagate Heavenly Bamboo by division.

Catmint *(Nepeta mussinii)*

Related to Catnip *(N. Cataria)*, Catmint has square stems and aromatic evergreen leaves that are heart shaped, toothed, and hairy. Tubular, blue, ½-inch flowers are clustered around the stems in 6-inch spikes in late spring and early summer. The gray-green plants grow 2 feet tall and spread in a mounded shape to 2 feet across. 'Blue Wonder', pictured here, has 1½-inch leaves and lavender-blue flowers.

GROWING TIPS

Grow Catmint in full sun in any well-drained garden soil; it likes poor, dry soil best. After Catmint flowers, cut the plants back to keep them compact and to encourage a second flowering. The plants should also be cut back in early spring to improve their appearance. Catmint can be invasive and, like Catnip, may attract cats. Propagate new plants by division or from seeds.

Sundrops *(Oenothera tetragona)*

Sundrops are day-blooming members of the genus that includes the evening primroses. This species grows 1–2 feet high and is usually woody at the base. The stems are reddish, and the lance-shaped leaves are shiny green and 1–2 inches long. The cup-shaped yellow flowers, which bloom in early summer, have 4 petals and are 2 inches wide.

GROWING TIPS

Grow Sundrops in full sun in open, sandy or average, well-drained soil. It grows in moist soil and also tolerates dry and poor soil. Sundrops spreads quickly and may need yearly dividing or thinning in spring or fall. New plants can be grown from seeds.

Mondo Grass (*Ophiopogon japonicus*)

Mondo Grass has tufts of dark green, arching leaves that are 8–16 inches long and ⅛ inch wide. They grow thickly from the base of the plant. Loose, erect clusters of nodding, pale lavender flowers bloom in summer; they are often hidden by the foliage. Blue berries form after the flowers. Mondo Grass spreads by underground stolons to form a 6- to 12-inch-high ground cover.

GROWING TIPS

Mondo Grass tolerates a wide range of light conditions, from full sun to shade. In very hot climates, protect it from direct sun, especially in the afternoon. Mondo Grass also tolerates heat, seashore conditions, and a wide range of soils. Cut back or mow Mondo Grass in the spring if the leaves become unattractive over the winter. Propagate new plants by division.

Prickly Pear *(Opuntia humifusa)*

Prickly Pear is one of the few members of the cactus family that will withstand frost. It has flat, spiny segments or pads that are oval or oblong and 2–6 inches long. The plants spread horizontally along the ground. Yellow, 2- to 3-inch flowers bloom on short, conical stems in early summer. Green to purple, oval fruits appear in fall; they are edible but not tasty. Prickly Pear is sometimes sold as *O. compressa* or *O. vulgaris.*

GROWING TIPS

Plant Prickly Pear in full sun and sandy, dry, well-drained soil. It is very drought tolerant and must not be over-watered. To propagate Prickly Pear, break off one of the segments and root it in sand or grow new plants from seeds. Plant this spiny plant in an area with little foot traffic and always wear gloves when you handle it.

Canby Paxistima (*Paxistima canbyi*)

Zone 5

Canby Paxistima, sometimes called Rat-Stripper, grows 1 foot high and spreads 3–5 feet across. Wiry stems root as they grow along the ground. The fine-textured, evergreen leaves are narrow and ½–1 inch long. They are shiny and medium green, turning bronzy in the fall. The flowers, which are reddish, are tiny and somewhat inconspicuous. They bloom in mid-spring to early summer. Canby Paxistima is a very neat plant and is at home in a rock garden or a low border.

Growing Tips

Canby Paxistima grows in full sun or partial shade. It grows best in moist, sandy, rich, slightly acid soil but will grow in any soil as long as it is well drained. It likes high humidity but will not tolerate excessive summer heat. It needs freezing temperatures during the winter. Propagate Canby Paxistima by division, by layering, or from stem cuttings.

Jerusalem Sage *(Phlomis fruticosa)*

A shrubby perennial or small shrub, Jerusalem Sage is somewhat coarse looking and is best suited to the informal garden. It has many branches that grow from 2–4 feet high and are covered with yellow, matted hairs. The oval, wrinkled leaves grow 4 inches long. Rounded whorls of 2-lipped yellow flowers bloom in early summer.

GROWING TIPS

Plant Jerusalem Sage in full sun and dry, infertile, well-drained soil. Remove flowers as soon as they fade to encourage a second bloom. In fall, cut the plant back by a third to keep it compact and give it shape. Propagate new plants from seeds or cuttings or by division.

Moss Pink *(Phlox subulata)*

Sometimes called Mountain Pink or Ground Pink, Moss Pink is an evergreen that grows 6 inches high. The stems grow rapidly and root as they creep along the ground, forming a dense, mossy mat 2 feet across. The leaves of Moss Pink are needlelike and 1 inch long. The ¾-inch flowers have 5 notched petals and may be white, rose, pink, red, lavender, purple, or blue. Moss Pink blooms in clusters in mid-spring to late spring. Trailing Phlox, *P. nivalis,* is another low-growing phlox that likes full sun.

GROWING TIPS

Moss Pink needs full sun to grow at its best, and it prefers average, well-drained soil. After the plants flower, shear them back to keep them compact. Moss Pink is subject to mildew; locate it in a place with good air circulation. Propagate new plants from cuttings, by division, or from seeds.

Dwarf Japanese Fleece-Flower
(Polygonum cuspidatum compactum) Zone 4

Dwarf Japanese Fleece-Flower grows 2–3 feet high and spreads by underground stems to 4 feet across. Its stiff, angled stems have obvious swollen joints, similar to those of bamboo, and sometimes have brown spots or streaks. The oval, 3- to 6-inch leaves are pale green, changing to red in the fall. The ¼-inch pink flowers bloom in spikes from the leaf axils in late summer, followed by red or pink seed heads. This species is sometimes called *P. reynoutria.*

GROWING TIPS
Plant Dwarf Japanese Fleece-Flower in sun in any dry, well-drained soil. It will grow anywhere and is very invasive, so plant it in a large area. To keep it contained, grow it in a pot set into the ground or surround it by an underground barrier. Propagate new plants by division or from seeds.

Spring Cinquefoil (*Potentilla tabernaemontani*)

Spring Cinquefoil is an evergreen plant that grows 3–4 inches high and rapidly spreads to 1½–2 feet across. Its horizontal branches root easily as they grow along the ground. The bright green leaves have 5 toothed, hairy leaflets; each about ¾ inch long. The single, ½-inch flowers are golden yellow and have prominent stamens. They bloom in small, loose clusters in late spring. This plant is sometimes sold as *P. verna*.

GROWING TIPS

Plant Spring Cinquefoil in full sun; if you give it some shade it will tolerate high summer heat. It prefers dry, fertile, well-drained soil but does not mind poor soil. In early spring, cut Spring Cinquefoil plants back or mow them to encourage dense new growth. Start new plants from cuttings, by division, or from seeds.

Three-toothed Cinquefoil
(Potentilla tridentata)

The leaves of Three-toothed Cinquefoil, often called Wineleaf Cinquefoil, are divided into 3 shiny, dark green leaflets that turn deep red in the fall. The plants are evergreen and grow 6–9 inches tall, spreading slowly to 2 feet across. The branches are woody and root as they grow along the ground, forming a loose mat. Small, 5-petaled white flowers with prominent stamens bloom in clusters in early summer. The variety 'Minima' grows only 3 inches high.

GROWING TIPS

Three-toothed Cinquefoil grows best in full sun, but it likes partial shade where summers are hot. It prefers dry, fertile, well-drained soil but tolerates poor soil. Start new plants from cuttings, by division in spring or fall, or from seeds.

Fragrant Sumac (*Rhus aromatica*)

Fragrant Sumac grows 1–5 feet high and spreads to 6 feet across. The aromatic leaves have 3 coarsely toothed, oval leaflets. The leaflets, which are each 2–3 inches long, turn bright red or orange in the fall. Before the leaves open in spring, spikes of single, greenish-yellow flowers bloom. Small, hairy, red berries form in clusters in fall. The variety 'Gro-Low', pictured, grows only 2 feet high. Unlike its close relatives, Poison Ivy and Poison Sumac, Fragrant Sumac does not cause a skin rash. It is sometimes called *R. canadensis*.

GROWING TIPS

Fragrant Sumac likes full sun and average, well-drained garden soil but will tolerate poor, dry soil. It grows best if it is watered frequently during the summer. Use it on slopes where erosion control is needed, in wide borders, or at the seashore. Propagate new plants by division, from root cuttings, or from seeds.

Rose Acacia *(Robinia hispida)*

Rose Acacia, or Pink Locust, is a deciduous, spreading shrub that grows 3–4 feet high. Its branches are brittle and covered with red bristles. The leaves are divided into 7–13 leaflets, which are oval to round and 1 inch long. Pink or rose-colored flowers bloom in sparse, nodding clusters in early summer. Because it spreads by underground stolons, Rose Acacia is a good choice for slopes that need erosion control.

GROWING TIPS

Plant Rose Acacia in full sun. It prefers moderately fertile soil but will often thrive in poor, sandy soil. New plants can be propagated by dividing the stolons, but they are usually grown from seeds.

Memorial Rose *(Rosa wichuraiana)*

Memorial Rose, the parent of numerous modern climbing roses, is a ground-hugging or trailing species rose that grows to 1½ feet high. It has strong, hooked thorns on its branches. There are 7–9 shiny, rounded leaflets per leaf; each one is ¾–1 inch long. The fragrant, white flowers, which are single and measure up to 2 inches across, bloom in clusters in early summer; there is no repeat bloom. The red fruits, called hips, are egg shaped and ½ inch long.

GROWING TIPS

Plant Memorial Rose in full sun in rich, well-drained soil. Prune the oldest canes (branches) to the ground each year to promote new growth and give the plant shape. Leaving the hips on all winter will increase the plant's hardiness. Propagate Memorial Rose from stem cuttings.

Trailing Rosemary
(*Rosmarinus officinalis* 'Prostratus')

Trailing Rosemary is an evergreen shrub that grows 6–24 inches high and spreads 4–6 feet across. Its branches root as they creep along the ground. The needle-like, aromatic leaves, which are ½–1 inch long, are shiny gray-green on the upper surfaces and woolly and white on the undersides. Small, fragrant, pale blue flowers bloom in upright spikes in late winter to late spring, depending on the climate.

GROWING TIPS

Trailing Rosemary likes full sun and average, dry soil that is well drained. It is very tolerant of heat, drought, and poor soil, and grows well without water or fertilizer (but if you want to use it as an herb, it should have slightly moist and fertile soil). Cut Trailing Rosemary back after it has flowered to keep it neat and to prevent excess woodiness. Propagate new plants from cuttings, by division, or by layering.

Rue *(Ruta graveolens)*

A shrubby evergreen, Rue has deeply cut, blue-green leaves that are highly aromatic. Clusters of buttonlike, yellow flowers bloom in clusters in early summer to midsummer on 1½- to 3-foot stems. Rue is often grown in low hedges and borders for its attractive foliage, which can be dried. If you desire foliage only, shear off the flower buds as they form.

GROWING TIPS

Plant Rue in full sun and poor, moist, well-drained soil. Do not fertilize it. In spring, cut the plants back to keep them compact. The foliage of Rue can cause an allergic reaction, so wear gloves when handling it. Give Rue winter protection in the colder limits of its hardiness. Plants can be increased by division or from seeds.

Lavender Cotton *(Santolina)*

A mounded, aromatic evergreen, Lavender Cotton *(S. chamae-cyparissus)* grows rapidly to 1–2 feet high and 2–3 feet across. Its woolly foliage is silvery gray, and its golden-yellow flowers are ¾ inch across and bloom on 6-inch stems in summer. It is sometimes sold as *S. incana*. Green Lavender Cotton *(S. virens)*, pictured, has finely divided, dark green leaves. It grows more slowly than its relative but reaches the same size. It has creamy-yellow, buttonlike flowers in summer at the top of leafless, 6- to 10-inch stems. This species is also called *S. viridis*.

GROWING TIPS

Both lavender cottons grow in full sun in any dry, infertile, well-drained soil; both are very tolerant of heat and drought. Propagate new plants by cuttings or by division. Shear lavender cotton plants when necessary to keep them compact.

Rock Soapwort *(Saponaria ocymoides)*

Rock Soapwort is a trailing plant that grows 4–8 inches high and has slender stems that can spread to several feet across. The lance-shaped leaves are downy and semievergreen. The 5-petaled, ½-inch flowers, which bloom in early summer in dense clusters, are bright pink or white. The ends of the petals are fringed or notched. Use Rock Soapwort as a ground cover or let it cascade from the top of a wall.

GROWING TIPS

Rock Soapwort is easy to grow in full sun and sandy or average, well-drained garden soil. After the plants have bloomed, cut them back to encourage compact growth. Propagate new plants by dividing the roots in spring or fall, from cuttings, or from seeds.

Yellow Stonecrop *(Sedum reflexum)*

Zone 5

A succulent evergreen, Yellow Stonecrop grows 3 inches high and up to 15 inches across. The branches are densely covered with fleshy, gray-green leaves. The golden-yellow flowers are star shaped and bloom in clusters in summer at the top of 12-inch stems.

GROWING TIPS

Yellow Stonecrop grows best in full sun. The soil should be sandy, poor, and dry; excellent drainage is necessary, especially in winter. Stonecrop spreads rapidly but is easy to weed out because it has shallow roots. Propagate Yellow Stonecrop from stem or leaf cuttings, by division, or from seeds.

Pork and Beans (*Sedum* × *rubrotinctum*) Zone 8

Pork and Beans is a creeping, slow-growing evergreen that grows 8 inches high. It roots at the stem joints as it grows along the ground. The cylindrical leaves are ½ inch long and densely crowded on the branches. In full sun, the leaves turn bronzy red and look something like baked beans. Small, yellowish-red flowers bloom in clusters in spring. This plant is particularly attractive in a rock garden, where the rocks will set off its unusual foliage.

GROWING TIPS

Pork and Beans is easy to grow in well-drained garden soil in full sun or light shade. Good drainage is important, especially in winter. Propagate the plants from seeds, by division, or from leaf and stem cuttings.

Bumald Spirea (Spiraea × bumalda) Zone 4

Bumald Spirea is a deciduous shrub that grows to 3 feet high and spreads to 5 feet wide. The twigs are striped and are covered with toothed, oval to lance-shaped leaves. Tiny flowers bloom in 4- to 6-inch clusters in midsummer to late summer. Two common cultivars with bright crimson flowers are 'Froebelii' (pictured), which is slightly taller than the species, and 'Anthony Waterer', which is more compact. Bumald Spirea is a welcome addition to the late summer garden when few other ground covers are in bloom.

GROWING TIPS

Plant Bumald Spirea in full sun to partial shade in soil that is moist and well drained. It is an adaptable shrub that will withstand less than ideal growing conditions. Prune the stems back to the ground in early spring before growth starts to ensure a compact habit. Start new plants from cuttings, by layering, or from seeds.

Lamb's-Ears *(Stachys byzantina)*

Lamb's-Ears has soft, white, woolly leaves, which are oval and 4 inches long. The foliage grows on spreading stems to form a mat that is 8 inches high and 3 feet across. Tubular, inch-long flowers bloom in whorled spikes in summer on 18-inch stems. The flowers may be pink or purple. 'Silver Carpet', shown here, does not flower, but it makes a denser, more compact ground cover. Lamb's-Ears is ever-green in zones 8–10. It is some-times sold as *S. lanata* or *S. olympica*.

GROWING TIPS

Plant Lamb's-Ears in full sun and average soil that has good drainage, especially during the winter. In early spring, cut back leaves that were damaged over the winter. When Lamb's-Ears becomes over-crowded, divide the plants in early spring or fall. Grow new plants from seeds in early spring.

Cutleaf Stephanandra
(Stephanandra incisa 'Crispa') Zone 4

An arching, deciduous shrub with drooping stems, Cutleaf Stephanandra is used as a ground cover or broad hedge in vast spaces or on slopes. The variety 'Crispa' grows 1½–3 feet high. The pointed, oval leaves are 2–2½ inches long with toothed lobes. In fall, the foliage turns reddish purple. Greenish-white, cup-shaped flowers bloom in clusters 1½–2½ inches long in late spring.

GROWING TIPS
Plant Cutleaf Stephanandra in full sun in average, well-drained garden soil. Trim the plants in early spring if they need shaping. They can be propagated from cuttings or by dividing clumps in early spring.

Cushion Japanese Yew
(*Taxus cuspidata* 'Densa')

Cushion Japanese Yew is a coniferous evergreen with 1-inch, dark green needles and reddish-brown branches. It is a dense, rounded shrub, 1½ feet high and 3 feet across. Female plants produce toxic red berries; the leaves and bark are also toxic. 'Prostrata', another low Japanese Yew, grows 1½–2 feet high, spreads to 4 feet across, and has a flat top.

GROWING TIPS
Yews grow best in full sun and moist, fertile, neutral to acid soil that is well drained. Cushion Japanese Yew will not grow in constantly wet soil or in hot and dry climates. It needs protection from winter sun and wind. Propagate yews from cuttings or seeds.

Wall Germander *(Teucrium chamaedrys)* Zones 5–6

Wall Germander grows 10–12 inches high and spreads by underground stems to 2 feet across. The shiny, dark green leaves are toothed and up to ¾ inch long. The leaves and stems are covered with white or silver hairs. In summer, loose, showy spikes of tubular, 2-lipped flowers appear. The flowers are white, purple, or pink. The variety 'Prostratum', pictured, grows only 6 inches high and 2 feet wide.

GROWING TIPS

Wall Germander will grow in full sun or light shade in any well-drained garden soil. Water the plants deeply but infrequently. They should be planted away from drying winds and need winter protection in colder areas. In early spring, prune away any branches damaged during the winter. Wall Germander can be sheared and is often used as a neat edging or a border plant in formal gardens. Propagate new plants from cuttings, by division, or from seeds.

Woolly Thyme *(Thymus pseudolanuginosus)*

Woolly Thyme creeps along the ground and forms a shrubby mat ½–1 inch tall and 1½ feet wide. Its soft, gray, oval leaves are hairy and aromatic. The stems are also gray and hairy. Woolly Thyme rarely flowers, but when it does, the flowers are pink and bloom in summer.

GROWING TIPS

Plant Woolly Thyme in full sun and poor, dry soil with good drainage. It is very tolerant of high summer heat. Woolly Thyme tolerates light foot traffic and is often planted between stepping stones. It can also be used in rock gardens or as a border plant. Propagate new plants from cuttings, by division, or from seeds.

Creeping Thyme is a shrubby mat-forming perennial that grows 1–2 inches high and spreads to 1½ feet across. The aromatic, evergreen leaves are narrow, leathery, and only ¼ inch long. The ½-inch flowers are white, pink, rose, purple, or red and bloom in summer in rounded or hemispherical clusters. The flowering stems are 4 inches high. Some botanists believe that this is the same plant as *T. praecox arcticus,* Mother-of-Thyme, which looks identical.

GROWING TIPS

Creeping Thyme shows off its foliage and flowers to their best when it is allowed to grow over and around rocks. It can also be used as a border plant or a lawn substitute. Plant it in full sun and dry, poor, well-drained soil. Creeping Thyme tolerates drought and summer heat. New plants are grown from cuttings, by division, or from seeds.

Low-Bush Blueberry (*Vaccinium angustifolium*) Zone 3

Low-Bush Blueberry is a twiggy, deciduous shrub that grows 1–2 feet tall. The leaves are small, narrow, and elliptic; they turn bright red in the fall. The small, urn-shaped flowers, which bloom in the spring, are often inconspicuous. They are white and sometimes have reddish lines. The ½-inch, edible fruit is blue-black.

GROWING TIPS

Plant Low-Bush Blueberry in full sun for the best berry production. It prefers sandy, rich, acid soil but will tolerate dry soil. It also withstands high summer heat. Propagate new plants from stem cuttings or by division.

Mountain Cranberry
(Vaccinium vitis-idaea minus)

Mountain Cranberry is a shrubby evergreen that grows 6 inches high and spreads from 15–30 inches across by creeping roots. The upright branches are covered with oval, shiny, ½- to 1-inch leaves. Small, urn-shaped, pink flowers bloom in nodding clusters in late spring. They are not particularly showy. In fall, red berries appear; they are edible but sour.

GROWING TIPS
Mountain Cranberry likes full sun and sandy, rich, moist, acid soil. Propagate new plants from cuttings, by layering, or by division.

Verbena *(Verbena peruviana)*

One of about 200 species of verbena, this makes an excellent ground cover. It grows 3–4 inches high; its stems root at the nodes as they creep along the ground to form a dense mat. The oblong, dark green leaves are rough to the touch and deeply toothed. Small, tubular, bright red flowers bloom in early summer in rounded clusters. There are hybrids with flowers of white, pink, rose, and purple.

GROWING TIPS

Select a spot for *V. peruviana* in full sun and dry, well-drained soil. Dry banks and rock walls are excellent locations. Once established, these plants are drought tolerant. Prune them in the fall to promote dense growth. In colder zones, this verbena can be grown as an annual. Propagate new plants from seeds in early spring or by cuttings taken in the fall.

Rock Speedwell *(Veronica prostrata)*

Rock Speedwell is a tufted or mat-forming plant. It has small, narrow, linear leaves and showy blue flowers, which bloom in spikes at the ends of erect, 8- to 10-inch stems in late spring and early summer. There are varieties with white and pinkish-purple flowers; 'Rosea' is pictured. Rock Speedwell is a relative of Creeping Speedwell, *V. repens,* which tolerates foot traffic but can become a lawn weed.

GROWING TIPS

Rock Speedwell grows in full sun or partial shade in average to rich soil that is moist and well drained. Its growth is denser in full sun. To grow new plants, divide existing plants after they have flowered, take stem cuttings, or start from seeds.

APPENDICES

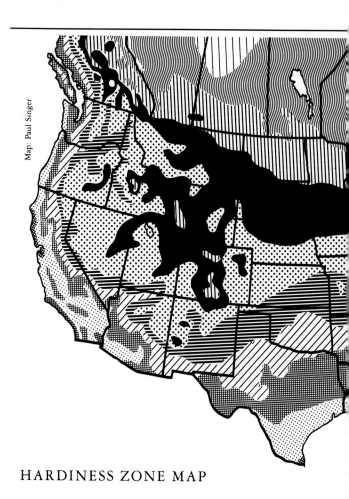

Map: Paul Singer

HARDINESS ZONE MAP

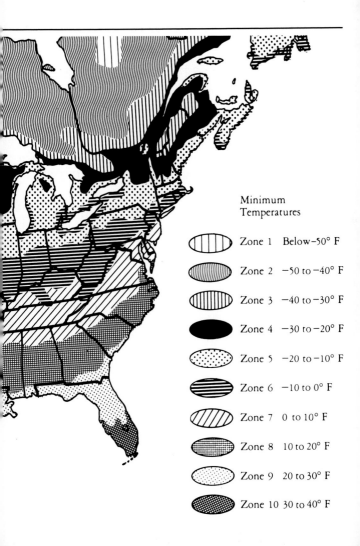

Minimum
Temperatures

Zone 1   Below −50° F

Zone 2   −50 to −40° F

Zone 3   −40 to −30° F

Zone 4   −30 to −20° F

Zone 5   −20 to −10° F

Zone 6   −10 to 0° F

Zone 7   0 to 10° F

Zone 8   10 to 20° F

Zone 9   20 to 30° F

Zone 10 30 to 40° F

GARDEN PESTS AND DISEASES

PLANT PESTS and diseases are a fact of life for a gardener. Therefore, it is helpful to become familiar with common pests and diseases in your area and to learn how to control them.

Symptoms of Plant Problems

Because the same general symptoms are associated with many diseases and pests, some experience is needed to determine their causes.

Diseases

Both fungi and bacteria are responsible for a variety of diseases ranging from leaf spots to wilts to root rot, but bacterial diseases usually make the affected plant tissues appear wetter than fungi do. Diseases caused by viruses and mycoplasma, often transmitted by aphids and leafhoppers, display such symptoms as mottled yellow or deformed leaves and twisted or stunted growth.

Insect Pests

Numerous insects attack plants. Sap-sucking insects—including aphids, leafhoppers, and scale insects—suck plant juices. The affected plant becomes yellow, stunted, and misshapen. Aphids and scale insects produce honeydew, a sticky substance that attracts ants and sooty mold fungus growth. Other pests with rasping-sucking mouthparts, such as thrips and spider mites, scrape plant tissue and then suck the juices that well up in the injured areas.

Leaf-chewers, namely beetles and caterpillars, consume plant leaves, whole or in part. Borers tunnel into shoots and stems, and their young larvae consume plant tissue, weakening the plant. Some insects, such as various grubs and maggots, feed on roots, weakening or killing the plant.

Nematodes

Microscopic roundworms called nematodes are other pests that attack roots and cause stunting and poor plant growth. Some kinds of nematodes produce galls on roots, while others produce them on leaves.

Environmental Stresses

Some types of plant illness result from environment-related stress, such as severe wind, drought, flooding, or extreme cold. Other problems are caused by salt toxicity, rodents, birds, nutritional deficiencies or excesses, pesticides, or damage from lawn mowers. Many of these injuries are avoidable if you take proper precautions.

Controlling Plant Problems

Always buy healthy disease- and insect-free plants, and select resistant varieties when available. Check leaves and stems for dead areas or off-color and stunted tissue. Later, when you plant your ground covers, be sure to prepare the soil properly.

Routine Preventives

By cultivating the soil routinely you will expose insects and disease-causing organisms to the sun and thus lessen their chances of surviving in your garden. In the fall, be sure to destroy infested or diseased plants, remove dead leaves and flowers, and clean up plant debris. Do not add diseased or infested material to the compost pile. Spray plants with water from time to time to dislodge insect pests and remove suffocating dust. Pick off the larger insects by hand. To discourage fungal leaf spots and blights, always water plants in the morning and allow the leaves to dry off before nightfall. For the same reason, provide adequate air circulation around leaves and stems by spacing plants properly.

Weeds provide a home for insects and diseases, so pull them up or use pre-emergent herbicides (we do not recommend the use of any other type). If you use weed-killers on your lawn, including "weed-and-feed" preparations, do not spray them near ground covers or apply them on a windy day. Herbicide injury may cause leaves to become elongated, straplike, or downward-cupping.

Insecticides and Fungicides

To protect plant tissue from injury due to insects and diseases, a number of insecticides and fungicides are available. However, few products control diseases due to bacteria, viruses, and mycoplasma. Pesticides are usually either "protectant" or "systemic" in nature. Protectants keep insects or disease organisms away from uninfected foliage, while systemics move through the plant and provide some therapeutic or eradicant action as well as protection. Botanical insecticides such as pyrethrum and rotenone have a shorter residual effect on pests but are considered less toxic and generally safer for the user and the environment than inorganic chemical insecticides. Biological control through the use of organisms like *Bacillus thuringiensis* (a bacterium toxic to moth and butterfly larvae) is effective and safe.

Recommended pesticides may vary to some extent from region to region. Consult your local Cooperative Extension Service or plant professional regarding the appropriate material to use. Always check the pesticide label to be sure that it is registered for use on the pest and plant with which you are dealing. Follow the label concerning safety precautions, dosage, and frequency of application.

GLOSSARY

Acid soil
Soil with a pH value lower than 7.

Alkaline soil
Soil with a pH value of more than 7.

Annual
A plant whose entire life span, from sprouting to flowering and producing seeds, is encompassed in a single growing season.

Axil
The angle formed by a leafstalk and the stem from which it grows.

Basal leaf
A leaf at the base of a stem.

Biennial
A plant whose life span extends to two growing seasons, sprouting in the first growing season and then flowering, producing seed, and dying in the second.

Blade
The broad, flat part of a leaf.

Bract
A modified and often scalelike leaf, usually located at the base of a flower, a fruit, or a cluster of flowers or fruits.

Bud
A young and undeveloped leaf, flower, or shoot.

Bulb
A short underground stem, the swollen portion consisting mostly of fleshy, food-storing scale leaves.

Clasping
Surrounding or partly surrounding the stem, as in the base of the leaves of certain plants.

Compound
Similar parts aggregated into a whole, as in a compound leaf, composed of two or more leaflets.

Creeping
Prostrate or trailing over the ground or over other plants.

Cross-pollination
The transfer of pollen from one plant to another.

Crown
That part of a plant between the roots and the stem, usually at soil level.

Cultivar
An unvarying plant variety maintained by vegetative propagation rather than from seed.

Cutting
A piece of plant without roots; set in a rooting medium, it develops roots and is then potted as a new plant.

Deciduous
Dropping its leaves; not evergreen.

Dissected leaf
A deeply cut leaf; same as a divided leaf.

Division
Propagation of a plant by separating it into two or more pieces, each of which has at least one bud and some roots.

Double-flowered
Having more than the usual number of petals, usually arranged in extra rows.

Drooping
Pendant or hanging, as in the branches of a weeping willow.

Evergreen
Retaining green leaves on one year's growth until after the new leaves for the subsequent year have been formed.

Fertile
Bearing both stamens and pistils; able to produce seed.

Fruit
The fully developed ovary of a flower, containing seeds.

Genus
A group of closely related species; plural, genera.

Germinate
To sprout (applied to seeds).

Hardwood cutting
A cutting taken from a dormant plant after it has finished its yearly growth.

Heel
The base of a plant cutting or tuber used for propagation, often with some of the old stock attached.

Herbaceous perennial
A plant whose stems die back to ground level each fall, but that sends out new shoots and flowers for several successive years.

Horticulture
The cultivation of plants for ornament or food.

Humus
Partly or wholly decomposed vegetable matter, an important constituent of garden soil.

Hybrid
The offspring of two parent plants that belong to different species, subspecies, genera, or varieties.

Invasive
Aggressively spreading from the original site of planting.

Irregular flower
A flower with petals that are not uniform in size or shape; such flowers are generally bilaterally symmetrical.

Lance shaped
Shaped like a lance; several times longer than wide, pointed at the tip and broadest near the base.

Layering
A method of propagation in which a stem is pegged to the ground and covered with soil and thus induced to send out roots.

Leaflet
One of the subdivisions of a compound leaf.

Leaf margin
The edge of a leaf.

Loam
A humus-rich soil containing up to 25 percent clay, up to 50 percent silt, and less than 50 percent sand.

Lobe
A segment of a cleft leaf or petal.

Lobed leaf
A leaf whose margin is shallowly divided.

Midrib
The primary rib or midvein of a leaf or leaflet.

Mulch
A protective covering spread over the soil around the base of plants to retard evaporation or control temperature.

Neutral soil
Soil that is neither acid nor alkaline, having a pH value of 7.

Node
The place on the stem where leaves or branches are attached.

Ovate
Oval, with the broader end at the base.

Panicle
An open flower cluster, blooming from bottom to top and never terminating in a flower.

Peat moss
Partly decomposed moss, rich in nutrients and with a high water retention, used as a component of garden soil.

Perennial
A plant whose life span extends over several growing seasons and that produces seeds in several growing seasons.

Petal
One of a series of flower parts lying within the sepals and outside the stamens and pistils; often large and brightly colored.

pH
A symbol for the hydrogen ion content of the soil, and thus a means of expressing the acidity or alkalinity of the soil.

Pistil
The female reproductive organ of a flower.

Pollen
Minute grains containing the male germ cells and produced by the stamens.

Propagate
To produce new plants, either by vegetative means involving the rooting of pieces of a plant, or by sowing seeds.

Prostrate
Lying on the ground; creeping.

Raceme
A long flower cluster on which individual flowers each bloom on small stalks from a common, large, central stalk.

Regular flower
A flower with petals and sepals arranged around the center, like the spokes of a wheel; always radially symmetrical.

Rhizome
A horizontal stem at or just below the surface of the ground, distinguished from a root by the presence of nodes and often enlarged by food storage.

Rootstock
The swollen, more or less elongate, underground stem of a perennial herb; a rhizome.

Rosette
A crowded cluster of leaves; usually basal, circular, and at ground level.

Runner
A prostrate shoot, rooting at its nodes.

Seed
A fertilized, ripened ovule, naked in conifers but covered with a protective coating and contained in a fruit in all other garden plants.

Semievergreen
Retaining at least some green foliage well into winter, or shedding leaves only in cold climates.

Sepal
One of the outermost series of flower parts, arranged in a ring outside the petals, and usually green and leaflike.

Simple leaf
A leaf with an undivided blade; not compound or composed of leaflets.

Softwood
Green wood at an intermediate growth stage.

Solitary
Borne singly or alone; not in clusters.

Species
A population of plants or animals whose members are potentially able to breed with each other, and that is reproductively isolated from other populations.

Spike
An elongated flower cluster whose individual flowers lack stalks.

Spine
A strong, sharp, usually woody projection from the stem or branches of a plant.

Stamen
The male reproductive organ of a flower.

Sterile
Lacking stamens or pistils and therefore unable to produce seeds.

Stolon
A horizontal stem, just above or beneath the soil, from the tip of which a new plant arises; a runner.

Stratify
To keep seeds under cool, dark, moist conditions to encourage them to break dormancy and germinate after treatment.

Subshrub
A partly woody plant.

Subspecies
A naturally occurring geographical variant of a species.

Succulent
A plant with thick, fleshy leaves or stems that contain abundant water-storage tissue. Cacti and stonecrops are examples.

Taproot
The main, central root of a plant.

Terminal
Borne at the tip of a stem or shoot, rather than in the axil.

Toothed
Having the margin divided into small, toothlike segments.

Tuber
A swollen, mostly underground stem that bears buds and serves as a storage site for food.

Variegated
Marked, striped, or blotched with some color other than green.

Variety
A population of plants that differs consistently from the typical form of the species, occurring naturally in a geographical area. Also applied, incorrectly but popularly, to forms produced in cultivation.

Vegetative propagation
Propagation by means other than seed.

Whorl
A group of three or more leaves or shoots that emerge from a stem at a single node.

PHOTO CREDITS

INDEX

Acacia, Rose, 86

Achillea tomentosa. 26

Alyssum saxatile. 34

Antennaria
   dioica. 27
   dioica rosea. 27

Anthemis nobilis. 45

Arabis. 28
   caucasica. 28
   procurrens. 28

Arctostaphylos uva-ursi. 29

Arctotis. 30

Arenaria montana. 31

Armeria maritima. 32

Artemisia stellerana. 33

Aurinia
   saxitilis. 34
   saxitilis 'Citrina', 34

Baby's-Breath, Creeping, 62

Baccharis
   pilularis. 35
   pilularis 'Twin Peaks', 35

Bamboo, Heavenly, 74

Barberry, Warty, 36

Basket-of-Gold, 34

Bearberry, 29

Bellflower, 40

Berberis verruculosa. 36

Bluebeard, 41

Blueberry, Low-Bush, 101

Broom, 60

Bruckenthalia spiculifolia. 37

Calluna
   vulgaris. 38
   vulgaris 'J. H. Hamilton', 38

Campanula
   carpatica. 39
   elatines garganica. 40

Candytuft, Perennial, 66

Caryopteris
   × *clandonensis*. 41
   × *clandonensis* 'Blue Mist', 41
   × *clandonensis* 'Kew Blue', 41

Catmint, 75

Ceanothus, Point Reyes, 42

Ceanothus gloriosus. 42

Cerastium tomentosum. 43

Ceratostigma plumbaginoides. 44

Chamaemelum nobile. 45

Chamomile, Roman, 45

Cinquefoil
   Spring, 83
   Three-toothed, 84
   Wineleaf, 84

Cistus × *pulverulentus*. 46

Coronilla
   varia. 47
   varia 'Penngift', 47

Cotoneaster
  Bearberry, 48
  Rock, 49
  Rockspray, 49
Cotoneaster
  dammeri. 48
  dammeri 'Skogsholm', 48
  horizontalis. 49
Coyote Brush, Dwarf, 35
Cranberry, Mountain, 102
Cranesbill, Pyrenean, 61
Cress
  Rock, 28
  Wall, 28
Cypress
  Russian, 73
  Siberian Carpet, 73

Daboecia
  cantabrica. 50
  polifolia. 50
Daisy, African, 30
Daphne, Rose, 51
Daphne
  cneorum. 51
  cneorum 'Eximea', 51
Dianthus gratianopolitanus. 52
Duchesnea indica. 53
Dusty Miller, 33

Erica
  carnea. 54
  carnea 'Springwood Pink', 54
Eriophyllum, Woolly, 55
Eriophyllum lanatum. 55

Euphorbia, Myrtle, 56
Euphorbia myrsinites. 56

Fleece-Flower, Dwarf Japanese, 82
Forsythia, Bronx Greenstem, 57
Forsythia viridissima 'Bronxensis', 57
Fragaria chiloensis. 58

Gaultheria shallon. 59
Genista pilosa. 60
Geranium
  endressii. 61
  endressii 'A. T. Johnson', 61
  endressii 'Wargrave Pink', 61
Germander, Wall, 98
Gypsophila
  repens. 62
  repens 'Rosea', 62

Harebell, Carpathian, 39
Heath
  Irish, 50
  Spring, 54
Heather, 38
Helianthemum
  nummularium. 63
  nummularium 'Raspberry
    Ripple', 63
Herniaria glabra. 64
Holly, Japanese, 67
Hypericum calycinum. 65

Iberis
  sempervirens. 66
  sempervirens 'Autumn Snow', 66

sempervirens 'Snowflake', 66
Ilex
  crenata. 67
  crenata 'Helleri', 67
  crenata 'Repandens', 67

Juniper
  Japanese, 69
  Shore, 68
Juniperus
  conferta. 68
  conferta 'Blue Pacific', 68
  procumbens. 69
  procumbens 'Nana', 69

Kinnikinick, 29

Lamb's-Ears, 95
Lantana, Weeping, 70
Lantana montevidensis. 70
Lavandula
  angustifolia. 71
  angustifolia 'Hidcote', 71
  angustifolia 'Munstead', 71
Lavender, English, 71
Lavender Cotton, 90
  Green, 90
Leadwort, 44
Leiophyllum
  buxifolium. 72
  buxifolium prostratum. 72
Locust, Pink, 86

Menziesia polifolia. 50
Microbiota decussata. 73

Mondo Grass, 77
Mother-of-Thyme, 100
Myrtle
  Allegheny Sand, 72
  Sand, 72

Nandina domestica 'Harbor
  Dwarf', 74
Nepeta
  mussinii. 75
  mussinii 'Blue Wonder', 75

Oenothera tetragona. 76
Ophiopogon japonicus. 77
Opuntia
  compressa. 78
  humifusa. 78
  vulgaris. 78

Paxistima, Canby, 79
Paxistima canbyi. 79
Phlomis fruticosa. 80
Phlox, Trailing, 81
Phlox
  nivalis. 81
  subulata. 81
Pink
  Cheddar, 52
  Ground, 81
  Moss, 81
  Mountain, 81
Polygonum
  cuspidatum compactum. 82
  reynoutria. 82
Pork and Beans, 93
Potentilla

tabernaemontani, 83
tridentata, 84
tridentata 'Minima', 84
Prickly Pear, 78
Pussytoes, 27

Rat-Stripper, 79
Rhus
  aromatica, 85
  aromatica 'Gro-Low', 85
  canadensis, 85
Robinia hispida, 86
Rockrose, Hybrid, 46
Rosa wichuraiana, 87
Rose
  Memorial, 87
  Rock, 63
Rosemary, Trailing, 88
Rosmarinus officinalis 'Prostratus', 88
Rue, 89
Rupturewort, 64
Ruta graveolens, 89

Sage, Jerusalem, 80
St. Johnswort, Aaronsbeard, 65
Salal, 59
Sandwort, Mountain, 31
Santolina, 90
  chamaecyparissus, 90
  incana, 90
  virens, 90
  viridis, 90
Saponaria ocymoides, 91
Sedum
  reflexum, 92

× *rubrotinctum*, 93
Snow-in-Summer, 43
Soapwort, Rock, 91
Speedwell
  Creeping, 104
  Rock, 104
Spike-Heath, 37
Spiraea
  × *bumalda*, 94
  × *bumalda* 'Anthony Waterer', 94
  × *bumalda* 'Froebelii', 94
Spirea
  Blue, 41
  Bumald, 94
Stachys
  byzantina, 95
  byzantina 'Silver Carpet', 95
  lanata, 95
  olympica, 95
Stephanandra, Cutleaf, 96
Stephanandra incisa 'Crispa', 96
Stonecrop, Yellow, 92
Strawberry
  Beach, 58
  Mock, 53
  Sand, 58
Sumac, Fragrant, 85
Sundrops, 76

Taxus
  cuspidata 'Densa', 97
  cuspidata 'Prostrata', 97
Teucrium
  chamaedrys, 98
  chamaedrys 'Prostratum', 98

Thrift, Common, 32
Thyme
  Creeping, 100
  Woolly, 99
Thymus
  praecox arcticus, 100
  pseudolanuginosus, 99
  serpyllum, 100

Vaccinium
  angustifolium, 101
  vitis-idaea minus, 102
Verbena, 103

Verbena peruviana, 103
Veronica
  prostrata, 104
  prostrata 'Rosea', 104
  repens, 104
Vetch, Crown, 47

Wormwood, Beach, 33

Yarrow, Woolly, 26
Yew
  Cushion Japanese, 97
  Japanese, 97